Pausing With God

Sheri Powell

SLP COMPANY
Sharing the Lord with People

Cover designed by David Humphrey - www.seehmg.com
Book edited by Sherrie Clark (SV.Clark@comcast.net)
Published by: SLP Company, P.O. Box 9172, Fleming Isle, FL 32006
Printed by: Quad Graphics www.QG.com
Registered with the Library of Congress Case Number: 1-466304512
ISBN: 978-0-615-42112-4

You can contact the SLP Company or Sheri Powell at:
www.PausingWithGod.com
Email: info@PausingWithGod.com
Write us at:
SLP Company
P. O. Box 9172
Fleming Isle, FL 32006

Printed in the United States of America
First Printing: 12/2010

DEDICATED TO THE
MEMORY OF MY MOTHER,
DELORISE SIMMONS,
"A WOMAN OF EXCELLENCE."

What other readers have said about *Pausing With God*...

"Sheri has an anointed message divinely given to her for the sole purpose of relieving, comforting, restoring, and inspiring women before, during, and after menopause."

Cleo D. Graham, R.N.P., B.S.N.,M.N.

What's absolutely clear to me after reading Pausing With God (although I already knew it) is how you so love the Lord! It's a truth that resonates with every turn of the page. I commend you my sister, for your persistent resolve to put to pen what has been bottled up in your heart.

Joleen Green
Bridgeport, Ct

I was amazed at the level of faith this woman of God has, but she doesn't hesitate to share an honest human side of herself. Author Sheri Powell's clever use of analogies and scriptures prepares the readers for each section and each point. Pausing With God has humor and wisdom…a good mixture for an easy-to-read book.

Sherrie Clark
Writer & Editor

ACKNOWLEDGMENTS

First, I must thank God because of what He has done, is doing and has promised to do in His Word. I have truly tasted and seen that He is good. (Psalm 34:8 KJV)

God's love, mercy and grace are everlasting! Without Him, none of this would be possible. But with Him, all things are possible! (Matthew 19:26 KJV)

Second, I must express my heartfelt gratitude to my family and friends. Your love and support has allowed me to be all that God has created me to be.

Third, I'd like to take a few lines to thank all the women who God has placed in my life. There are too many to name here because I have had many teachers, cheerleaders and Bible study buddies. You have physically and spiritually been my Aaron and my Hur.

Some days you have walked along side of me and others you pushed me forward, helping me become who I am today. Thank You!

Next, I want to thank Sherrie Clark, my editor and Dave Humphrey, the most awesome graphic arts designer and consultant. You are the best Lamaze partners. Thank you for helping me birth this baby!

And lastly, THANK YOU for choosing this book, and I pray you enjoy *Pausing With God*!

FOREWORD

A foreword can be written in many different formats. As I pondered who to ask, I was told that I should try to speak to a well-known person, one who is an expert on the subject matter.

The foreword is an important part of a book. It helps you decide whether or not you want to continue. So in preparation, I moved forward and sought the Lord as to who He wanted to participate with this section.

The response that leaped in my heart was the first and the last. Selah. I paused and thought about this for almost an hour. I then envisioned my oldest and youngest child as the authors of the foreword.

What a perfect answer. I couldn't have thought of this myself. Who knows me better than they do? Who else has first-hand knowledge of my journey with menopause but them?

- Sheri Powell

My knowledge of menopause is limited since I have yet to experience it. Observing the effects of menopause in my mother's life has taught me a few things and given me a sense of confidence that when it's my season, I will not be afraid.

Whether or not you decide to treat menopause with supplements or medicines is a personal choice. However, as a woman of God, having faith in Him is a must during menopause. My wish is for you, the reader, to gain a different perspective about menopause and to know that you're not alone.

- Synora W. McCoy

When my mom asked me to make a contribution in the foreword, my first response was, "I didn't even know you were writing a book." But after reading the first chapter, I wanted to let you know that this book was written by an inspired woman who cares not only about her own well-being, but about the well-being of others, too.

I acquired lots of memories while discovering the good news about this book, too many to put to paper, but I believe she has designed a road map through menopause.

I can't say that it is easy, me not being a woman, but as my mom explains, menopause is not something you can get through on your own. If you let God guide you through this trying time, it will be less difficult.

I encourage women to read this book and keep an open mind in order to obtain new information about menopause that you might not have previously known.

-     Joseph N. Powell

INTRODUCTION

Because of this book's subject matter, there would normally be in-depth medical terminology and a doctor's synopsis. Instead of following tradition, Pausing With God will take a different approach.

This book was written to provide you with laughter, a teary eye and a resolve that you will make it as you journey through your season of menopause.

Whether you are premenopause, perimenopause, meno-pausal, postmenopause or too young to even think about it, my prayer is that you will be encouraged in a way that you never imagined possible.

My hope is that this book provides you with a sense that you are not alone in this emotional, mental, physical and spiritual passage of menopause.

This book is NOT intended to be used for medical advice, or to diagnose, or to cure and/or to prevent menopause. Because there are numerous indicators and tests used to determine the season of menopause you may be in, seeing someone in the medical profession would be in your best interest.

**This book has been written as an
instrument of encouragement.**

TABLE OF CONTENTS

CHAPTER ONE

Menopause

BLESSED BE GOD, EVEN THE FATHER
OF OUR LORD JESUS CHRIST,
THE FATHER OF MERCIES, AND THE
GOD OF ALL COMFORT;
WHO COMFORTETH US IN
ALL OUR TRIBULATION,
THAT WE MAY BE ABLE TO COMFORT
THEM WHICH ARE IN ANY TROUBLE,
BY THE COMFORT WHEREWITH
WE OURSELVES ARE COMFORTED OF GOD.
FOR AS THE SUFFERINGS OF
CHRIST ABOUND IN US,
SO OUR CONSOLATION ALSO
ABOUNDETH BY CHRIST.

2 CORINTHIANS 1:3-5 (KJV)

J ust the mere mention of the word *menopause* has possessed such a negative undertone in the past. I believe this is because it was so misunderstood. But thank goodness there is a great deal of information, treatment and therapy available for women today. We no longer have to suffer in silence.

I can remember hearing stories from elderly women about the "dark tunnel" and how they had no hope of returning back to normal. Their tales frightened me to the point that I blocked the reality that one day I too would have to walk through this season.

Regardless, the cycle of menopause is inevitable for all women. One thing I've discovered is that we need the grace of God and *one another* to walk this journey victoriously. The purpose of this book is to encourage you that menopause is not the end of the world nor is it a "dark tunnel of no return." Menopause is a season of preparation and perfecting. God has us in the palms of His hands, and it is He who will minister, deliver, heal, comfort and set us free. Hmm…

even in the midst of menopause? Yes, even in the midst of menopause, for we are just merely taking a *pause* for a season.

Jeremiah 1:5 (paraphrased) reminds us that everything we have gone through (our past), are going through (our present) and will go through (our future), God knew about it before we came out of our mother's womb. God said He sanctified us and ordained us to know that there is nothing—no circumstance—that can touch us without Him knowing about it first. And since He knew it, there must be some great purpose in it for His glory and our benefit. So be encouraged as we are **Pausing With God**, the Father of our Lord and Savior Jesus Christ, and trust that He will give us exactly what we need.

Thoughts & Reflections

Thoughts & Reflections

CHAPTER TWO

Conditioning

AND NO MAN PUTTETH NEW WINE
INTO OLD BOTTLES,
ELSE THE NEW WINE DOTH
BURST THE BOTTLES,
AND THE WINE IS SPILLED,
AND THE BOTTLES WILL BE MARRED;
BUT NEW WINE MUST BE
PUT INTO NEW BOTTLES.

MARK 2:22 (KJV)

Conditioning

If you don't know how a home air conditioning system operates, you'll find out when yours ceases to work. To my surprise, I found an air conditioning unit to be nothing more than a piece of metal whose sole purpose is to provide comfort for us by moving hot air from the inside-out.

Occasionally, the coils in our unit would freeze. The first thing we did when our unit lost its cooling capacity was to turn it off. In the meantime, we made an attempt to remain cool with window fans.

On this most recent incident, by day-three; we thought it might be a good time to call a repairman. The technician inspected the unit and advised us that the entire system would need to be replaced.

Seeing what your home is really made of while being gutted is amazing. After the old unit was taken out, the technician further discovered that the foundation it rested upon was not secure. This project had become more involved than we had anticipated.

Inside the house with the electricity

9

completely off, the technician moved quickly, for the "natives were getting restless." Once everything was installed, we were ready to pop open the champagne, but a wrench was thrown into our plans. The technician stated that when a new unit is installed, having the air ducts vacuumed and checked for M & M's (mold and mildew) is highly recommended as a final step.

I couldn't identify with this extra step. Where we grew up, the maintenance crew never cleaned our air ducts. Oh, I forgot. Perhaps it was because we didn't have central air back in those days.

During this experience, however, the Lord revealed that our bodies are similar to an air conditioning unit. There can be various reasons why they cease to work efficiently. We can become too busy tending to everyone else that we forget to take care of ourselves. As long as our bodies rise up and get going every day, we fail to check to see if our filters are clogged and if our ducts need to be vacuumed.

In our journey through menopause, we won't be successful if we only
try to clean the outside. God's way is
from the inside-out. Depending on how
long we have rested on the old foundation, we may have to be gutted before
the new one can be laid.

We can't move into all that God
has for us if we're carrying our old ways
and old habits. It's no longer business
as usual. The old self has been stretched
to the limit and worn out. If God was to
pour into us without any inner change,
we wouldn't be able to handle it.

So be encouraged as the conditioning begins. Keep in mind that God is
preparing us for what is ahead.

Conditioning

Thoughts & Reflections

Thoughts & Reflections

Thoughts & Reflections

CHAPTER THREE

Half-Time

"THE GLORY OF THIS LATTER HOUSE
SHALL BE GREATER THAN OF THE FORMER,"
SAITH THE LORD OF HOSTS,
"AND IN THIS PLACE WILL I GIVE PEACE,"
SAITH THE LORD OF HOSTS.

HAGGAI 2:9 (KJV)

For most of us, a large span of our lives, time and energy have been invested in spouses, children, families, friends, jobs, church and other extracurricular activities. Don't get me wrong. These investments are important. But women tend to put themselves on the "back burner" while the demands, expectations and responsibilities of others monopolize their time.

Menopause is a time in our lives when we are to take all the experiences and celebrate how far we have come, who were are, and where we are headed. The season of menopause enables us to take an honest look at our lives and come up with a game plan for the second half.

I'm not a big football fan, but like most, eating snacks and watching the commercials keep me occupied until the half-time show. A game of football is parallel to our lives. In the beginning we come out of the locker room full of energy and excitement. By half-time, we have figured-out that we can't expect to win the game using the strategies from our old playbooks if we are the losing team.

Half-Time

Half-Time

On December 28, 1996, I and two other women received a word of prophecy: "In this prophecy, you will not hear the words *soon* or *about,* but you will hear the words *this very day.*

"In 1987, the New York Giants were heavy favorites to defeat the Denver Broncos in the Super Bowl. But when the first half was over, they went into the locker room downcast, dejected and disappointed because they were losing this battle 10 to 9. And this is pretty much the way this Christian walk has gone for the three of you up to this point. You have won some battles and lost some battles. You have won some fights but lost some fights. You have won a few skirmishes but lost a few skirmishes while the devil has continued to maintain a slight advantage over your heads.

"But when the intermission was over, and the Giants came out for the second half, there was a fire in their eyes and a burning in their hearts. And <u>in the second half alone, they dominated, destroyed and defeated their enemy.</u>

18

*They turned a narrow defeat into a
victorious celebration. And as it was with
them, so shall it be with you.*

"For our sovereign Lord would
have me say unto the three of you
this very day, 'The first half is over.
Intermission is now over. And the second
half is now, has now, shall now and will
now commence!'"

I am convinced that we must let
God give us His strategy that is needed
for the second half of our lives. With His
way, we win the championship.
Are you looking forward to a day when
you can have that victory Jesus is talking
about? Do you even realize that it's
yours? Take God at His Word, and do not
let the opposing team's score discourage
you. If God said it, it is so!

You are in the game of life,
and there are two teams. It is you and
menopause, which is challenging by no
stretch of the imagination. You will at
times go kicking, carrying or handing off
an attitude or action that is not becoming
of you. Menopause has the ability to put
you in one of the following situations:

Half-Time

Half-Time

an incomplete pass, a fumble, and/or running out-of-bounds. Any one of these plays can put you on the loser's side or the winner's side. The question is, which side do you want to be on?

Beginning right now, I pray the Holy Spirit will liberally give each of us what we need to *dominate, destroy and defeat* everything that keeps us from having the winning strategy that's needed in our season of menopause.

Thoughts & Reflections

Thoughts & Reflections

CHAPTER FOUR

Pausing With God

NO MAN CAN SERVE TWO MASTERS:
FOR EITHER HE WILL HATE THE ONE,
AND LOVE THE OTHER...

MATTHEW 6:24 (KJV)

Menopause is a normal, natural event defined as the final menstrual period and usually confirmed when a woman has missed her periods for 12 consecutive months (in the absence of other obvious causes).[1] Menopause is associated with reduced functioning of the ovaries due to aging, resulting in lower levels of estrogen and other hormones. It marks the permanent end of fertility.

Most of us have probably received the warnings about the unpleasant chapters that we would face in life: puberty, adolescence, childbirth, and last but not least, menopause. In each one, we can find something that we all have in common. Each season is capable of teaching us an assortment of life-altering skills that if allowed, will prepare us for the next.

God wants us to discover and to follow His strategy as we pause in this latter season of our lives. We are to trust and obey Him, no matter what it looks like and no matter what we feel like. Never forget that He has us in the palms

Pausing With God

of His hands and that there is a purpose for this season.

Even when we lose our balance and take the wrong steps, our heavenly Father is there ready, willing and able to pick us up, dust us off and place our feet back on solid ground.

Speaking of solid ground. This was a place that I had yet to experience. Because of a number of female health problems, my physician recommended that I undergo a partial hysterectomy.

I was informed of the advantages and disadvantages of the procedure and the possible post-surgical risks, side effects and complications that could continue for several months to several years. Still, a period of unexpected events prevented me from connecting the symptoms that I was experiencing after the hysterectomy to that of early menopause. I summed it up to what was going on in my life; not with my body.

A short time later, I watched a close friend begin her expedition through menopause. She was one of the most encouraging and warm-spirited females I have ever met. She always had a smile and kind word for everyone. To me, she was the "Proverbs 31 woman" in-the-flesh, who we will discuss more in Chapter Eight.

I had been convinced that if anyone would gracefully dance through their season of change, it would be her. But as she began the journey, she was bamboozled by what was happening to her mind, body and soul. It affected her emotionally, physically and mentally in ways that she had never imagined.

Through the next couple of years in our time together, I looked for the woman I once knew. Her uncharacteristic responses to different situations in her life motivated me to make a conscious decision. I needed to prepare myself for when I would have my turn on the playing field. I would accept nothing less than *victory.*

I began to pray, expecting God to show up and help me every step of the way. I had a plan, and it was and

Pausing With God

still is to glorify Him in this area of my life.

One day unexpectedly, there came a knock on the door. Enter Mr. & Mrs. Mood Swings and their twins, Aches & Pains. They came carrying overnight bags which contained waves of fatigue, loss of energy, weight gain, depression, headaches, muscle pain, dry brittle nails, PMS symptoms, fluctuating body temperature, elevated cholesterol, allergies and some memory loss. I found out later that these were all symptoms associated with menopause.

During these times, I knew I needed to cry out to God for His love, mercy and grace. I would rise up early just so I could put forth the effort needed to make time for Him. At first, this was a struggle, but then I found it to be a privilege and a special time of sweet fellowship with the Lord.

Daily, God ministered and encouraged me with His word. One that still resonates in my spirit is, "'For

28

I know the thoughts that I think toward you,' saith the LORD, 'thoughts of peace, and not of evil, to give you an expected end. Then shall ye call upon me, and ye shall go and pray unto me, and I will hearken unto you. And ye shall seek me and find me when ye shall search for me with all your heart. And I will be found of you,' saith the LORD." (Jeremiah 29:11–14 KJV)

I love the way the Message Bible breaks it down. God will show up and take care of us as He has promised. He knows what He is doing. He has it all planned out—plans to take care of us, not to abandon us, plans to give us the future we hope for. When we call on Him, when we come and pray to Him, He'll listen. When we come looking for Him, we will find Him. Yes, when we get serious about finding Him and want it more than anything else, He'll make sure we won't be disappointed. We can count on it.

An expected end. I don't know about you, but that is confirmation from God. From Genesis to Revelation, God has shared with us what has happened,

Pausing With God

what is happening, and what will happen. In our relationship with God is where we will learn how to rest in His promises, in His provision and in His peace.

[1]The North American Menopause Society (cited with permission). "Menopause Glossary". Menopause, Menopause Information, About Menopause.
Updated 9/21/2010. http://www.menopause.org

Thoughts & Reflections

Thoughts & Reflections

CHAPTER FIVE

FOR I AM THE LORD, I CHANGE NOT...

MALACHI 3:6 (KJV)

Changes

The changes in our body have a tendency to trigger the way we feel, act and respond. One of my favorite sayings is, "What has our ATTENTION determines our ATTITUDE, which most of the time equals our ACTIONS."

When I was a teenager, I remember hearing warnings to be wary of a girl on her "monthly." She is someone to be reckoned with. Well that is putting it mildly, but you get the point. Now that I'm older, I hear the same being said about menopause. This excuse is frequently used when we find our emotions getting out of hand. We can make a big deal out of nothing by doing things we would not normally do and saying things we would not usually say.

We must be careful not to create a habit of excusing our behavior because of the way we feel. Let's do our best and remain accountable and responsible for our actions.

Changes

I knew something funny was going on with my body, but I couldn't put my finger on it. Anyone who knows me knows I love to talk.

One day I was in a conversation with some family members, and they began to irritate me in an unexplainable way. I looked at their faces. They were so animated, and their mouths appeared to be moving about 100 miles a minute. I couldn't make sense out of anything they said. All I heard was "blah, blah, blah!" Inside my core, there was a build-up of pressure that wanted to explode.

I know what you're thinking. We all feel like that every now and then. But this was a feeling that was not normal for me, and I didn't like it.

Accompanying the "blah, blah, blahs" were frequent dizzy spells. I didn't share this with anyone until one night after church when I went up for prayer. As they began to pray for me, I felt an instant release which I believe came from a combination of releasing it to God and sharing with a prayer partner.

Ladies, I want to encourage you
to find a prayer partner.

In May 2006, I made up my mind
to go to the doctor. It was funny how the
symptoms seem to subside as soon as
I made the appointment. I giggled and
thought about cancelling, but deep down
I knew that I needed to find out what
was going on.

I nervously explained my
symptoms to the doctor during my
examination. She listened patiently with
a smile on her face and intermittently
nodded her head. When I was done, she
looked over my chart and replied that
she had a clue as to what was happening.
She insisted on conducting some tests to
confirm her suspicions.

Weeks later, I went for my
follow-up visit to hopefully discover the
answers to all my questions. My wait in
the examination room seemed like an
eternity, although only five minutes had
passed.

My doctor entered the room

with a big grin on her face. She said with such coolness, "Guess what? You're smack-dab in the middle of menopause."

She began to explain that what I was going through was normal and encouraged me that it was just for a season.

We went over different types of medication and changes that could help me in this transition. She instructed me to go home and put my family on notice. This was my season, and it was time for *me* to take care of *me*.

I went home and made a list with three columns: what was important, what was urgent, and what was necessary. I made some lifestyle changes. I began to eat healthier, exercised frequently and tried to get at least eight hours of sleep each night.

I felt a new determination in my spirit. I felt like God was giving me a second chance and that He knew exactly what the outcome was going to be. He reminded me throughout His word that life will have its ups and downs, trials and tribulations, periods of sickness and health (seasons of puberty, adolescence, menstruation, and menopause), but through them all, He will give me everything that I need.

In Him and with Him, we can learn that menopause is just a PAUSE, preparing us for the next chapter of our lives. It's a time of switching from juggling everyone else's life to the balancing of our own.

Lord, help us emotionally, mentally, physically, and especially spiritually.

Thoughts & Reflections

Thoughts & Reflections

Thoughts & Reflections

CHAPTER SIX

Traffic

PRAY WITHOUT CEASING.

1 THESSALONIANS 5:17 (KJV)

I f you ever aspire to be a comedian and need an opening act, may I suggest the interaction between the people who are sitting in their cars while stuck in traffic? Cars jump in front of each other. People yell and make hand and facial gestures at one another. Being stuck in traffic obviously has the ability to create stressed and frustrated motorists.

I think to myself, *what are they accomplishing?* Absolutely nothing. If we are honest with ourselves, this is a waste of emotion and energy, and it keeps us from seeing hidden blessings.

There is a positive side of traffic jams. They make us slow down. Traffic jams don't have to be non-productive. We can use that time to see God in our day, to pray and to praise Him. When we begin to see from God's perspective, we will be mindful of events that we perceive as a nuisance.

Notice how menopause has been delayed and left for the latter part of

45

Traffic

our lives. Though all the symptoms and effects of menopause cause a traffic jam in our minds and bodies, we can find a positive side to it. Menopause is an event that fine-tunes us. It stops us and causes us to check our GPS and consider which way we're headed.

Remember, menopause is not here to destroy us but to perfect us. It can change our focus as we let God show us what is beyond the traffic jam.

Thoughts & Reflections

Thoughts & Reflections

CHAPTER SEVEN

Pattern

I CAN DO ALL THINGS THROUGH
CHRIST WHICH STRENGTHENETH ME.

PHILIPPIANS 4:13 (KJV)

When I met my husband, he was the one who came with a dowry. I was so excited when he came packing with a piece of furniture that I had always dreamed of having—a three-piece sectional living room set. When I laid my eyes on it, I was speechless. I was thinking *OMG. I haven't seen a design or color like this since back in the early 1970's—burnt orange, brown and beige with triangular geometric shapes.*

As we were getting settled in, the furniture found its home in the family room. Oftentimes I would stand afar trying to imagine its potential. In the meantime, I threw navy blue sheets over it to temporarily satisfy my frustration.

I made an appointment with a professional to obtain an estimate on what it would cost to upholster the furniture. I contemplated the price for a week or so. And then I remembered a similar piece of furniture my grandmother had in her living room when I was a teenager. I believe she had

Pattern

upholstered it all herself.

I telephoned Grandma and after catching up, we talked about how she created her masterpiece. I shared with her my blessing-in-disguise and asked her opinion. She advised me to upholster the sectional myself. She shared her wisdom and her confidence in me that I could and should embark on this project.

I had taken Sewing 101 in high school but nothing as large as what she suggested I do. So I began to pray and seek the Lord. In my prayer time, Philippians 4:13 rang in my ear, "I can do ALL things through Christ Jesus who strengthens me."

After a few additional calls to Grandma, I jotted down the three steps she provided:

1. Remove the original material from each piece of furniture.

2. Lay out each piece. This will be the pattern for the new material.

3. Pin the new material to the old and label each piece. Cut out the new pieces and began sewing.

52

I thought there had to be more to it than this. These three steps seemed so simple for a complex job. Whenever doubt crept upon me, I let God and Grandma's words replay in the back of my mind. Each day I began in prayer, asking the Lord for His wisdom, knowledge and understanding.

I understood that just knowing the basics wouldn't be enough to get me through. I went to the library and checked out a few how-to books and visited different stores collecting fabric samples and prices. My hearts desire for this project was to glorify God and benefit my family.

One night while window shopping, the Lord showered me with a blessing. I walked through a fabric store and saw that there just happened to be a 50%-off sale on upholstery fabric. This blessing couldn't get any better because the color of the fabric seamlessly matched the carpet in the family room.

Daily with pen and paper, I stopped and sought the Lord whenever I was stumped on how to proceed. As

He gave direction, I wrote them down. *Word of caution, be careful where you put notes-to-self.*

One day after school, the kids came home and saw my notes. They asked me who was I writing to, and why were the answers in my own handwriting. I told them what was going on, and they looked at me like I had lost my "marbles". It wasn't until a month later when the project had been completed that they realized how God uses the simple things to amaze the wise.

For years family and friends would visit, and they often commented on the furniture. We used that as an opportunity to give God the glory.

That furniture went on to be a blessing not only to my home, but to another household as well. We're not sure where this furniture is residing today, but if you happen to see a three-piece blue sectional and can pull up the fabric from the middle section in the back, you may see my kids' autographs.

Thoughts & Reflections

Thoughts & Reflections

CHAPTER EIGHT

Proverbs

MY PEOPLE ARE DESTROYED
FOR LACK OF KNOWLEDGE...

HOSEA 4:6

While raising our children, we tried to take every opportunity to point out God's handiwork. During bible studies together, we frequently visited the book of Proverbs. No matter how many times we perused this book, each time I came away with a greater appreciation for it.

God has given us instructions on how to conduct our lives in every circumstance and situation so that we may come "to know *wisdom* and instruction; to perceive the words of *understanding*; to receive the instruction of wisdom, justice, and judgment and equity; to give subtlety to the simple, to the young man, *knowledge* and discretion. A wise man will hear and will increase learning, and a man of understanding will attain wise counsel, to understand a proverb and the interpretation, the words of the wise and their dark sayings." (Proverbs 1:2-6)

All of God's word, when applied, can prepare and preserve us. But the first step is to actually read His Word and the second would be to

apply it. Solomon opens up the book of Proverbs stating specifically what it is all about: TO KNOW, TO PERCEIVE, TO RECEIVE, TO GIVE, and TO UNDERSTAND, if we are willing.

In elementary school, we learned about numerators and denominators. The numerator is the part of a fraction that is above the line and signifies the number to be divided by the denominator. The denominator is the part of a fraction that is below the line and which functions as the divisor of the numerator.

For mathematical sakes, we shall call ourselves the numerator and Proverbs the denominator. The denominator has three divisors: WISDOM, KNOWLEDGE and UNDERSTANDING. If we as the numerator apply the three divisors to our lives, we shall be those who are spoken about in Proverbs 1:33: "But whoso hearkeneth unto me shall dwell safely and shall be quiet from fear of evil."

You woke up and hopefully sprinkled your morning with a time of devotion with the Lord. Afterwards, you pull out your "To Do List". Seeing a day already filled with activity, you ponder where to begin.

Early afternoon you remembered that you invited some friends over for lunch but had forgotten to go to the store. You find yourself scrambling in the kitchen looking for something to prepare.

There's a knock on the door. Your guests arrive and notice your dilemma. They understand and do the wisest thing—open your fridge and cupboards. They then proceed to create precious memories and an unbelievable meal. You exhale in awe of their understanding and wonder why you spent so much energy fussing over nothing.

Ladies, on our journey with menopause, we will have moments where we just can't get it or keep it

all together. But we must allow God's Word to encourage us so that we can move on to encourage one another. No matter what goes on during our day, when we tap into God's three ingredients, He will give us a recipe that will surely be a hit.

We women must educate ourselves and not rely on old wives tales that were handed down from one generation to another. We need WISDOM on how we are to conduct our lives, UNDERSTANDING on how our bodies work, and the KNOWLEDGE that can help us apply it to be the best that we can be.

It doesn't matter if you are single, married, divorced or widowed, the illustration given to us in Proverbs 31:10-31 is a model of a truly good woman. She is not meant to appear perfect. But this chapter provides us with an example from which we can gleam; it gives us a glimpse of our capabilities.

"For who can find a virtuous woman? For her price is far above rubies." (Proverbs 31:10 KJV). The Merriam Webster dictionary defines virtuous as "having or exhibiting virtue, morally excellent."

A Proverbs woman and a ruby are alike. Both are very rare, precious and expensive. In making them, their creators begin with their imperfections. Endurance and patience are required as they undergo extreme makeovers and numerous treatments.

They will be cut, put through the fire, and polished as they pass through the trials and tribulations of life. In their cooling-down periods, you will notice their appearance has been radically changed. From this point forward, they must be handled with care and protected. Though they are desired for their toughness and inner beauty, their surface is still subject to damage. But once the process is complete, they are flawless and their value never decreases.[2]

Proverbs

Notice that the woman in Proverbs 31:10-31 is an action woman. She provides a pattern for us, one that shows creativity, productivity and resourcefulness. Each of us has been born with unique personalities, abilities and gifts. Amongst us are manufacturers, importers, managers, realtors, farmers, tailors, *upholsterers,* chefs, domestic engineers, merchants, overseers and so much more.

As we progress through our season of menopause, we must ask God to give us His wisdom, knowledge and understanding that will enable us to maintain an inner beauty. We will frequently have to pause with Him. Take inventory and find out what is important, what is urgent and only do what we can. God is going to be right there with us on this journey, and He will encourage us to live in fear of Him, not menopause.

[2]Wikipedia, The Free Encyclopedia. "Ruby". Ruby – Wikipedia, the free encyclopedia. Modified 9/24/2010. http://en.wikipedia.org/wiki/ruby

Thoughts & Reflections

Thoughts & Reflections

CHAPTER NINE

Acts

AND WHEN THEY HAD SET THEM IN
THE MIDST, THEY ASKED, "BY WHAT POWER,
OR BY WHAT NAME, HAVE YE DONE THIS?"

ACTS 4:7 (KJV)

After seeking the Lord for wisdom, knowledge and understanding, our next step is to put this into action. A good following to Proverbs is the book of Acts. In chapter four, we are told about the story of Peter and John as they faced opposition.

Menopause is our opponent. The parade of symptoms and complications can feel like our minds and bodies have been arrested. When we decide to take better care of ourselves, we become a threat to them. Sure, we'll have days where we won't feel like it. But if we can gather together and support one another, pressing into God's presence for His strength, we will begin to see that we can be made whole.

There are numerous other suggestions out there that may help you, but I know of no other way than to first try prayer, change our eating habits, exercise and fellowship. Being conscience of these four before, during and after a menopausal episode is imperative. Like anything else, moods

and all the other symptoms can trigger how often we pray, exercise and eat.

Before I encountered menopause, I sought God to prepare and instruct me on how this journey could bring Him glory. I had my share of Sadducees and high priests who neither agreed with nor understood my request.

But the more opposition I came across, the more I prayed. I read in God's Word and believed that we "can do all things through Christ which strengthens us," (Philippians 4:13) and that "with God nothing shall be impossible." (Luke 1:37)

I want to encourage you to take a step of faith and praise God when you are awaken by those night sweats. When you become moody, PAUSE and let God's love penetrate your heart. Gather together with some women of like-faith and have a praise-fest, seeking the Lord for the refreshing wind of the Holy Spirit, praying one another

through and claiming the promises of
God. Let's call down heaven right here
on earth.

Thoughts & Reflections

Thoughts & Reflections

Thoughts & Reflections

Chapter Ten

Titus

THE AGED WOMEN LIKEWISE, THAT THEY
BE IN BEHAVIOUR AS BECOMETH HOLINESS,
NOT FALSE ACCUSERS, NOT GIVEN TO
MUCH WINE, TEACHERS OF GOOD THINGS;
THAT THEY MAY TEACH THE YOUNG WOMEN
TO BE SOBER, TO LOVE THEIR HUSBANDS,
TO LOVE THEIR CHILDREN, TO BE DISCREET,
CHASTE, KEEPERS AT HOME, GOOD,
OBEDIENT TO THEIR OWN HUSBANDS,
THAT THE WORD OF GOD BE NOT BLASPHEMED.

TITUS 2:3-5 (KJV)

In the second chapter of Titus, Paul instructs the older women in Christ about their role and responsibility. He charges the women to disciple, teach, instruct and rebuke their generation.

However, I've noticed that from my conversations with women of all ages, there seems to be a decline with the performance of these functions in this present day. Receiving guidance from seasoned women is just as important today as it was in Paul's era.

We are to take Paul's admonishment seriously and communicate with the younger generation about every area of their lives. We not only need to prepare them for childhood, adolescence and young adulthood, but for womanhood as well.

Unfortunately, a number of women prior to my generation pressed through the different seasons of their lives with the playbook from their ancestors. Their daily responsibilities and duties were so overwhelming that they couldn't take the time to separate the

Titus

myths from the facts. They were simply too worn out because they had received some of the bad as well as the good advice, remedies and solutions.

Taking extra care of ourselves during menopause, also known as our "Titus season", is important. Yes, we are in a challenging place, but one that can benefit so many.

The younger generation is watching and can learn from our victories as well as our defeats. So no matter what age bracket you would categorize yourself, do not take lightly your God-given responsibility to the next generation.

While conducting research on this book, I approached several women and asked them to share their experiences with menopause. Many responded with some good advice and gave me their permission to pass them onto you:

"Remove yourself from others or simply don't speak when the irritation sets in. You can hurt others when there is absolutely nothing they are doing. Get LOTS of exercise; it helps the most with everything to do with menopause."
Pamela Carden

"ANYTHING you get from the other ladies…pass it on – pass it on!!!! LOL. I have officially gone 2 ½ months without a cycle, and the increase of the hot flashes has been HORRIBLE!

"I noticed that when I had cut back to only one cup of coffee, I didn't experience them as often. I also have to drink plenty of water after work until it's time for bed to soothe the hot flashes during the night.

"As soon as I feel that hotness, I immediately start with the fan for air (take something with me everywhere for that). If I catch it soon enough, it doesn't take over my entire body. I

also notice that I get them when I am anxious or stressed.

"And the dreadfulness of working out! If I don't want to work out but do anyway, I do not have a single hot flash. NOT ONE! Just 30 minutes of working out has helped a lot.

"Thank GOD I don't have the emotional part of it such as crying at anytime or yelling at everyone around me. I think I've become much more carefree, but I will tear-up easily.

"I was talking to my granddaughter's grandmom about menopause yesterday after work. I told her that no matter what I get—hot flashes, pimples, fat, whatever—it sure beats having a cycle! LOL.

"She was rolling! She asked, 'Your cycles were that bad?'

"'Nah…not at all. They just annoyed me. I don't like being annoyed anymore in life.'

"My doctor (male if you can believe that) is an advocate of no drugs and no surgery for anything, so he just listens to me and tells me to increase my vitamins, etc. Black Cohash worked right away for me as well, but about a week later, I had horrible rashes all over my arms and neck.

"So...sigh. That was history. He tells me every year that he never would have tied my tubes after my last child. Said that's messing with the body's creation, thus, open to cause problems. LOL!

"It's God's body, and I know we will not know why he made it this way until we are with Him. Well...sure we won't care then." *Angela Dowdy-Reid*

"I had an ablation 3 years ago. I elected to do the ablation because my periods were becoming very heavy and irregular. Now I do not have one, but I experience the symptoms of having a period. I bloat, crave salt, chocolate, experience tenderness, cry and suffer from low back pain. I am 49, and some-times I feel like 50. I am going through

Titus

so many changes, it is hard to tell what is what. Raising my granddaughter is such a blessing because she keeps me so busy. I can blame all of my tiredness on her. I do know that when I eat right, get enough sleep, exercise and worship, I feel much better. This takes discipline which I lack. So please pray for me to have more discipline in my life. Love You. God Bless." *Karen Beck*

"A lot of mood swings and depression. Sometimes I am glad I live alone so no one will notice my crying spells. Also, I am battling with my weight. It is a hot mess! Oh, did I forget to mention the hot flashes." *Laverne Davis*

Thoughts & Reflections

Thoughts & Reflections

CHAPTER ELEVEN

Psalms

THE LORD IS MY SHEPHERD; I SHALL NOT WANT.
HE MAKES ME TO LIE DOWN IN GREEN PASTURES;
HE LEADS ME BESIDE THE STILL WATERS.
HE RESTORES MY SOUL;
HE LEADS ME IN THE PATHS OF
RIGHTEOUSNESS FOR HIS NAME SAKE.
YEA, THOUGH I WALK THROUGH
THE VALLEY OF THE SHADOW OF DEATH,
I WILL FEAR NO EVIL; FOR YOU ARE WITH ME;
YOUR ROD AND YOUR STAFF, THEY COMFORT ME.
YOU PREPARE A TABLE BEFORE ME IN
THE PRESENCE OF MY ENEMIES;
YOU ANOINT MY HEAD WITH OIL;
MY CUP RUNS OVER. SURELY GOODNESS AND
MERCY SHALL FOLLOW ME ALL THE DAYS OF MY LIFE;
AND I WILL DWELL IN THE
HOUSE OF THE LORD FOREVER.

PSALMS 23:1-6 (KJV)

When I was in junior high and high school, only the odd-numbered questions and answers were printed in the back of my math textbooks. Well, we have all the questions but not all the answers. God's Word (the Bible) has all the questions and all the answers. He tells us over and over again what He has done, is doing and shall do for us.

No matter what menopause challenges we are facing today, we must keep our mind on His promises. Post them up as a reminder on our bathroom mirror or as a screensaver on our computer monitor. Better yet, do we have the nerve to purchase some sidewalk chalk to write His answers in our driveways?

I love the story of the two sisters, Martha & Mary, found in Luke 10:38-42. Martha worried about what was not getting done. Getting things done was her priority; her relationship

Psalms

with Jesus came second. She was busy doing this and doing that, trying to impress Him.

On the other hand, Mary found it a privilege and honor to sit at His feet, gaining what could never be taken away. Mary worshipped Jesus for what He had done. Her priority was to spend time with Him, and she sought intimacy with Jesus. She couldn't explain this kind of fellowship to Martha. It had to be experienced.

In our season of menopause, God's desire is not for us to be wandering around aimlessly or too busy to spend time with Him. He is our Shepherd and does not want to lose any of his sheep. He wants to guide us so that we will follow His plans and receive His blessings. In Him we have green pastures, still waters, restoration for our souls, paths of righteousness, a sense of peace, no fear of evil, comfort, a table of goodies, anointed heads, goodness and mercy till our cups are running over. And the best part is that we can have this ALL the days of our lives.

Below is a "Daily Reminder" assignment. Insert your name in the blanks and then read it aloud. Print it on your favorite stationary to serve as your daily reminder of what He has for you.

DAILY REMINDER

The LORD is _____ shepherd;

_____ shall not want.

He makes _____ to lie down in green pastures;

He leads _____ beside the still waters.

He restores _____ soul;

He leads _____ in the paths of

righteousness For His name sake.

Yea, though _____ walk through the valley

of the shadow of death,_____ will fear no evil;

For You are with _____;

Your rod and Your staff, they comfort _____.

You prepare a table before _____

in the presence of _____ enemies;

You anoint _____ head with oil;

_____ cup runs over. Surely goodness

and mercy shall follow _____ All

the days of _____ life; And _____

will dwell in the house of the Lord forever.

Psalms 23:1-6 (KJV)

Thoughts & Reflections

Thoughts & Reflections

Thoughts & Reflections

CHAPTER TWELVE

Ecclesiastes

LET US HEAR THE CONCLUSION
OF THE WHOLE MATTER:
FEAR GOD, AND KEEP HIS COMMANDMENTS:
FOR THIS IS THE WHOLE DUTY OF MAN.

ECCLESIASTES 12:13 (KJV)

Pausing *With God* has encompassed four sections. The first section included "Menopause", "Conditioning" and "Half-Time". The second section included "Pausing with God", "Changes" and "Traffic". The third included "Pattern", "Proverbs" and "Acts" and then concluded with "TitUs", "PSalms" and now "Ecclesiastes".

When we secure God's wisdom, knowledge and understanding (**Proverbs**) and apply it to our lives (**Acts**), God is able to USE (TitUs, PSalms and Ecclesiastes) us.

"In the sweat of thy face shalt thou eat bread, till thou return unto the ground; for out of it was thou taken: for dust thou art, and unto dust shalt thou return." (Genesis 3:19 KJV)

What do we gain from all our work day-in and day-out? The earth remains generation after generation; the wind blows one way only to return again. The rivers run into the sea, and

Ecclesiastes

yet it is never full. Wherever it came from, there it goes back. And so it is with us.

Have you ever wondered why we are here, why has God allowed us to see this day? There has to be at least one thing He desires for us to learn, to do, or just experience.

One morning 13 years ago on my way to work, I heard a children's story on the radio. The story was about two friends. One was a Christian, and the other wasn't.

The Christian went to church every week but didn't invite his friend. Sometime later, the non-Christian died in a house fire. He came back from the dead and visited the Christian.

He said, "I thought you were my friend?"

The Christian said, "Yes, I was."

The non-Christian sadly looked at the Christian and whispered, "If you were, then why didn't you tell me about Jesus? Why didn't you tell me that He could have saved my life?"

When this story went off the

air, I sat quietly in my car, and the Lord began to deal with me. He wanted me to use this tool as an opportunity to minister to one of my co-workers. You see, I was like the Christian friend who went to church every week and didn't invite my co-worker. As I got out of the car to enter my workplace, guess who pulled up? You betcha! My co-worker.

I was a little hesitant, but I recited the radio story to her anyway. Evidently, God's timing was perfect; she received the story as a message from the Lord.

Though each of us is different and has different needs, the fact remains that we will need each other more than ever in our season of menopause. We need to tell each other funny stories, silly jokes, and strategies of how we made it through some of the challenges we are facing.

We can strengthen one another on this journey. God is not allowing us to walk this way together for no reason at all. Share, for you may possibly save someone's life.

Where does pleasure and wealth really get you? So what. You get the promotion, more money, bigger home, newer clothes, fancy car and expensive furniture. What then? Solomon had it all. He built, planted, had servants and many possessions, but none of it satisfied him. He saw no gain and no purpose in any of these things.

I can relate to what Solomon was saying. When my mom was preparing to go to sleep to meet Jesus in 2008, I had to filter through her possessions. This was emotionally, mentally and physically challenging.

I remembered her telling our family years before she became ill, "Do not let Sheri give all my stuff away."

But when we had to release her personal effects, I gave them to all the ladies who had appreciated her taste and knew how much effort she put into each one of her possessions. You see, my mom had very exquisite taste. No matter

98

what she did or wore, it commanded a standing ovation.

The looks on the new owners' faces were similar to the expression on my mom's when she had first acquired them. This was a precious moment. I looked around, and I could see that even in her absence, my mom was still blessing so many.

I am persuaded that our lives, especially during our season of menopause, are for giving all we ever thought we were to God and allowing Him to give us all we will ever need. As He fills our empty spaces, He will remind us that these gifts are not for us to hang in a closet nor to be placed on a shelf or stuffed in a drawer. He is blessing us for us to simply be a blessing to others.

When I was a teenager, my dad once said. "A guy could sit on the stoop at night, and he gains a reputation. A girl sits on the same stoop at the same time,

and she loses her reputation."
It's not that she was doing anything wrong; it was simply the appearance that something was going on. Solomon, like my dad, stressed the importance of making the right choices.

Our everyday choices can affect our lives. There are some lifestyle changes that we will have to make for our journey with menopause to become easier. If we don't like to exercise alone, start a support group that walks together. If you have a problem eating late at night, try keeping nutritious snacks readily available. If you have a hard time sleeping, read your Bible.

No matter how long we live, we will be reminded that we have no control over some of the things that happen to us. No matter what we nip and tuck and take out or put in, our season of menopause is inevitable. Learning as quickly as possible to let go of what we can't control is in our best interest.

When I was a little girl living in a housing community, we didn't have to cut the grass; the maintenance people did it for us. Suffice it to say that when the Lord blessed me with a yard, I was an "eager-beaver" to keep it maintained.

One fine morning, the weather man said that a storm was coming in the afternoon. At the end of my work day, I glanced at the sky. It looked like I might have a good chance to cut the lawn. The sky was overcast with a slight breeze, providing the perfect grass-cutting conditions.

I began on one side of the house, and dark clouds were blowing my way quickly. I cut up and down and back and forth, each time peering up at the clouds and watching and waiting for the rain. Sometimes I tried to peek out of the corner of my eye as if God couldn't see me. I felt the Lord say, "Do not trust what you see, but have faith."

In spite of my weakness, the Lord was faithful, and I was able to get the entire yard done. No sooner had I

blown the last patch of loose grass from sidewalk did raindrops begin to fall upon my head. All I could do was look up and this time, it was with a thankful, not fretful, heart.

Then while studying the eleventh chapter of Ecclesiastes, God showed me verse four: "He that observeth the wind shall not sow; and he that regardeth the clouds shall not reap." The Lord reminded me that as long as I kept my eyes on the sky, I would not be able to finish what I started.

Ladies, in our season of menopause, God wants us to spend more time focusing on the positive and less on the negative. As Solomon echoed throughout Ecclesiastes, what will it profit us to gain the whole world, but lose our soul? What will it profit us to lose so much time by letting the negatives of menopause steal some of the best years of our lives?

Since you may never find the perfect timing or conditions to take care of you, don't wait until your symptoms have disappeared or your season of

102

menopause has ended. Menopause can take up to five years to complete and for some women, the process may take even longer. You will need creative strategies and reminders to help you through it. As you become aware of your triggers and monitor your lifestyle, look around your home. You probably have some things that you can use—maybe a small fan that you can duct-tape to the side of your nightstand, a back massager to alleviate the headaches, or manicure/ pedicure equipment to soothe away the grit of your day.

God doesn't want us confused and upset on this journey. He wants us to enjoy where we are, even if our forecast is stormy. While we may not know what is in store from hour to hour, we know the storekeeper, and His shelves are filled with nothing but good for us. God made us to bring Him glory. We only get one chance at it, so let's make the most of it.

Ecclesiastes

Last but not least, we cannot conclude without giving you, the reader, the opportunity to ask Jesus to be your personal Savior if you haven't done so already:

<u>Did you know that becoming a Christian is as easy as ABC?</u>

"For all have sinned, and come short of the glory of God." (Romans 3:23 KJV)

First, we have to **ADMIT** that we are a sinner and are willing to repent (turn) from it. Can we admit that something is missing in our lives? "But God commendeth His love toward us, in that while we were yet sinners, Christ died for us." (Romans 5:8 KJV)

Second, **BELIEVE** that Jesus died, was buried and rose from the grave for us. Do we believe that He died for us to bridge the gap in our relationship with God, mending that which had been broken by sin? "That if thou shalt confess with thy mouth the Lord Jesus, and shalt believe in thine heart that God hath raised Him from the dead, thou shalt be saved. For with the heart man believeth unto righteousness; and with the mouth confession is made unto salvation." (Romans 10:9-10 KJV)

Third, **CALL** on Jesus and invite Him into our lives to become our personal Savior. Are we are willing to exchange our will for God's will? "And it shall come to pass, that whosoever shall call on the name of the Lord shall be saved." (Acts 2:21)

If you are willing to say YES to all three of these, then my friend you are SAVED! Welcome into the family of God! If you have a special prayer request, pray the Lord's Prayer. As your will lines up with God's will, HE WILL work wonders.

The Lord's Prayer

OUR FATHER WHICH ART IN HEAVEN,
HALLOWED BE THY NAME.
THY KINGDOM COME, THY WILL BE DONE
IN EARTH AS IT IS IN HEAVEN.
GIVE US THIS DAY OUR DAILY BREAD.
AND FORGIVE US OUR DEBTS AS
WE FORGIVE OUR DEBTORS.
AND LEAD US NOT INTO TEMPTATION,
BUT DELIVER US FROM EVIL:
FOR THINE IS THE KINGDOM,
AND THE POWER, AND THE GLORY,
FOR EVER. AMEN.

MATTHEW 6:9-13 (KJV)

I pray that you daily R.S.V.P to your heavenly Father…as it is written, "Eye hath not seen, nor ear heard, neither have entered into the heart of man, the things which God hath prepared for them that love Him." (1 Corinthians 2:9 KJV)

Stay In His Will.

God Bless,
Your sister in Christ

Visit http://www.rbc.org for Daily Devotionals and for a full library of resources on living the Christian life which includes:

10 Reasons To Believe

Answers To Tough Questions

Been Thinking About

Christian Courses

Discovery Series

Help For My Life

Personal Relationship With God

Resources For Your Ministry

Strength For The Journey

Thoughts & Reflections

Thoughts & Reflections

Notes

1. http://www.merriam-webster.com/dictionary/sheep

2. http://www.merriam-webster.com/dictionary/virtuous

3. http://www.menopause.org/

4. http://en.wikipedia.org/wiki/Ruby

5. http://en.wikipedia.org/wiki/1987_Super_Bowl

6. http://en.wikipedia.org/wiki/Prophecy

7. http://www.menopause.org/MF200901two_menopausestatus.aspx

About the Author

Sheri Powell is well aware that menopause is a natural and inevitable time in a woman's life. She didn't realize that there was a way to walk through this season VICTORIOUSLY until she had to struggle with the symptoms herself.

Before coming to the Lord, she lived her life depending on other people to provide answers and solutions to the various dilemmas she would undoubtedly find herself. Even though she had occasionally visited various churches at a young age, she only came to know of the Lord. A relationship with Jesus Christ would not manifest until her adult years.

In the meantime, she grew up in a community housing area and took advantage of some of the benefits it provided. As a teenager, she tutored elementary school children, and her love for the younger generation blossomed.

Sheri fully surrendered to Jesus Christ on April 12, 1989. At that time, God began to give her beauty for ashes, the oil of joy for all her mourning, and the garment of praise for her heaviness. She became the planting of the Lord.

She then got involved in ministry as a children's church leader, "Inner-City Sidewalk" Sunday school teacher and as a youth group leader. For the past 10 years, she has served as a volunteer and mentor at a local Boys & Girls Club.

In 2001, Sheri and her family began utilizing the gifts and talents of the youth they mentored by hosting an annual "Mother & Daughter Prayer Breakfast". Soon after, the Lord enlarged her territory. He drew her to the parents of the children she mentored, particularly the mothers.

In July 2008, the Lord gave Sheri a vision of women "shutting-in" with Him. She inquired of the Lord, comparable to what Moses did in Exodus 3, 'Who am I, Lord, that I should go and gather a group of women together?"

The Lord reminded her of her aunt, First Lady Addie Stevens of Macedonia Church in Norwalk, Connecticut. For 20 years, Lady Stevens has been gathering women together, shutting-out the world and shutting-in with God for as long as two days.

Over the next two years, Sheri moved forward with the "shut-in" vision. She hosted 10 women's prayer "shut-ins". The first was 'Awake' where she and 35 women "shut-in" with God for two days. The next was a six-week Esther Bible Study, concluding with a One Night With A King celebration, followed by Walking Together in Prayer—Rejoice, Restoration and Revival, Judging Others, Our Defining Moment, Women Anointed in the Lord, The Tabernacle, In His Steps and Weeping Women of God.

Though Sheri possesses an Associate of Arts in Christian Counseling, she does not let degrees or titles define her. God has given her a slideshow of her life. In it, the Spirit of the Lord God is upon her, and the LORD has anointed her to preach good tidings unto the meek. He is sending her to bind up the brokenhearted, to proclaim liberty to the captives, to open the prison to them that are bound...and to comfort all that mourn. (Isaiah 61: 1-3 & Luke 4:18-19).

Sheri and her husband Anthony reside in Florida and live and breath to simply do God's will in sharing the good news about Jesus Christ. They have five adult children and a bouquet of family and friends.

To order send this completed order form to:

Pausing With God
C/O SLP Company
P. O. Box 9172
Fleming Isle, FL 32006

Date _____

Name _____

Mailing Address_____

City _____ State ____ Zip_____

I would like to order_____ Pausing With God book(s)

(Quantity)

$12.95 per book x _____ = $_____

(Quantity)   (Total of Order)

All Payments in US Dollars
(Price includes shipping & handling)

Credit Card Payment

Email address:_____

(If you are using a credit card we must have your email address)

○ Visa
○ Master Card
○ American Express

Card # _____

Expiration Date _____ Security Code _____

STANDARD SHIPPING:
Orders are shipped using the United States Postal Service's
Media Mail rate. Please allow 7-10 business days for your package to arrive.

Thank you for your order!